Open Access Scientific Repositories

First Edition

Ali I. Al-Mosawi

Shaymaa Abbas Abdulsada

Ph.D. Students in Faculty of Materials Science and Engineering, University of Miskolc, Hungary (2016-2020)

Preface.

This book includes lots of open access scientific repositories sites for universities and other scientific foundations, which contain thousands of theses, papers, and books in all humanitarian and scientific disciplines. Anyone can access to the locations of these repositories with ease and withdraw information he needs.

Title	**Scientific Open Access Repository of Portugal**
Description	RCAAP portal aims to collect, aggregate and index Open Access scientific contents from Portuguese institutional repositories. RCAAP constitutes a single entry point for searching, discovery and recall of thousands of scientific and scholarly publications, namely journal articles, conference papers, thesis and dissertations, distributed by several Portuguese repositories. A list of the repositories aggregated in the portal is available in the Directory. RCAAP portal is one of the main components from the project Repositório Cientfico de Acesso Aberto de Portugal. RCAAP project is an initiative from UMIC Knowledge Society Agency, developed by FCCN Fundação para a Computação Científica Nacional, with the technical and scientific collaboration from Minho University.
Website	http://www.rcaap.pt/

Title	**Brazilian Digital Library of Theses and Dissertations (BDTD)**
Description	The Brazilian Digital Library of Theses and Dissertations (BDTD) aims to integrate, in a single portal, theses information systems and existing dissertations in the country and available to users a national catalog of theses and dissertations in full text, allowing a only way to search and access to such documents. IBICT collects and makes available only the metadata (title, author, abstract, keyword, etc.) of theses and dissertations, and the original document remains in the defense establishment. Thus, the quality of the collected metadata and access to the full document are the sole responsibility of the home institution.
Website	http://bdtd.ibict.br/vufind/

Title	National Academic Research and Collaborations Information System (NARCIS)
Description	NARCIS is the main national portal for those looking for information about researchers and their work. Besides researchers, NARCIS is also used by students, journalists and people working in educational and government institutions as well as the business sector. NARCIS provides access to scientific information, including (open access) publications from the repositories of all the Dutch universities, KNAW, NWO and a number of research institutes, datasets from some data archives as well as descriptions of research projects, researchers and research institutes. This means that NARCIS cannot be used as an entry point to access complete overviews of publications of researchers (yet). However, there are more institutions that make all their scientific publications accessible via NARCIS. By doing so, it will become possible to create much more complete publication lists of researchers.
Website	http://www.narcis.nl/

Title	Cornell University Library (arXiv)
Description	Started in August 1991, arXiv.org (formerly xxx.lanl.gov) is a highly-automated electronic archive and distribution server for research articles. Covered areas include physics, mathematics, computer science, nonlinear sciences, quantitative biology and statistics. arXiv is maintained and operated by the Cornell University Library with guidance from the arXiv Scientific Advisory Board and the arXiv Member Advisory Board, and with the help of numerous subject moderators. Users can retrieve papers from arXiv via the web interface. Open access to 1,198,828 e-prints in Physics, Mathematics, Computer Science, Quantitative Biology, Quantitative Finance and Statistics.
Website	https://arxiv.org/

Title	DOepatents
Description	DOepatents, developed by the U.S. Department of Energy (DOE) Office of Scientific and Technical Information (OSTI), is a searchable database of patent information resulting from DOE-sponsored research and development (R&D). Included here are patents that DOE sponsored through a variety of funding mechanisms, including grants, contracts, or cooperative agreements. Comprehensive coverage of DOE patent information is one way to demonstrate the Department's contribution to scientific progress in the physical sciences and other disciplines. Publicly available patent information from DOE R&D, historic and current, is presented here, excluding patent applications. DOepatents consists of bibliographic records, with full text where available, either via a PDF file or an HTML link to the record at the United States Patent and Trademark Office (USPTO).
Website	http://www.osti.gov/doepatents/

Title	EScholarship University of California
Description	eScholarship provides a suite of open access, scholarly publishing services and research tools that enable departments, research units, publishing programs, and individual scholars associated with the University of California to have direct control over the creation and dissemination of the full range of their scholarship. With eScholarship, you can publish the following original scholarly works on a dynamic research platform available to scholars worldwide: Books, Journals, Working Papers, Previously Published Works, Conferences. eScholarship also provides deposit and dissemination services for postprints, or previously published articles. Publications benefit from manuscript and peer-review management systems, as well as a full range of persistent access and preservation services.
Website	http://escholarship.org/

Title	Electronic Theses of LMU Munich
Description	On this website you'll find currently 11883 electronic theses of the Ludwig-Maximilians-Universität München in PDF format. The University Library of the LMU Munich (Universitätsbibliothek) offers postgraduates the opportunity of submitting their theses in electronic form, provided that the Doctorate Regulations (Promotionsordnung) applicable to their subject contains an appropriate ruling.
Website	https://edoc.ub.uni-muenchen.de/

Title	JSTOR
Description	JSTOR is a digital library of academic journals, books, and primary sources. JSTOR helps people discover, use, and build upon a wide range of content through a powerful research and teaching platform, and preserves this content for future generations. JSTOR is part of ITHAKA, a not-for-profit organization that also includes Ithaka S+R and Portico. JSTOR goals: • Help scholars, researchers, and students discover, use, and build upon a wide range of scholarly content on a dynamic platform that increases productivity and facilitates new forms of scholarship. • Help libraries connect patrons to vital content while increasing shelf-space savings and lowering costs. • Help publishers reach new audiences and preserve their scholarly content for future generations.
Website	http://www.jstor.org/

Title	Erasmus University Thesis Repository
Description	The responsibility for the Thesis Repository is divided as follows: the faculties of the Erasmus University will deposit theses according to their own regulations; the RePub department of the University library provides the infrastructure, the hosting and the design of the workflows. The Faculty of Social Sciences (FSS), the Faculty of History and Arts (ESHCC), the Erasmus School of Economics (ESE) and the Institute of Health Policy and Management (iBMG) are already using the new thesis repository on a regular basis. Users can browse or search the repository, either in its entirety, or according to subdivisions, available through the navigation. The primary organization of the theses is by date, with the most recent ones shown first.
Website	https://thesis.eur.nl/

Title	Biskra University Theses Repository
Description	This platform allows you to access a part of the scientific production of the University of Biskra. You will find Doctoral Thesis. The scope of this platform will be soon enriched by memories of Magister and Master. To begin your search, select the "BROWSE" tab. You can search for a thesis based on certain criteria (simple and advanced search), or download existing theses (by year, by discipline, by author). Most theses are freely available. However, access to certain theses will be reserved for members of the University of Biskra or limited to only the summary document.
Website	http://thesis.univ-biskra.dz/view/divisions/

Title	University of Batna Theses Repository
Description	This platform allows you to access a part of the scientific production of the University of Batna (thesis, papers, and books).
Website	http://theses.univ-batna.dz/

Title	Middle East University Repository
Description	Offers the Middle East University thesis and papers.
Website	http://www.meu.edu.jo/ar/index.php?option=com_content&view=categories&id=156&Itemid=861

Title	Mohamed-Cherif Messaadia University - Souk Ahras Repository
Description	
Website	http://www.univ-soukahras.dz/en/publication

Title	The SAO/NASA Astrophysics Data System
Description	The SAO/NASA Astrophysics Data System (ADS) is a Digital Library portal for researchers in Astronomy and Physics, operated by the Smithsonian Astrophysical Observatory (SAO) under a NASA grant. The ADS maintains three bibliographic databases containing more than 12.3 million records covering publications in Astronomy and Astrophysics, Physics, and the arXiv e-prints. Abstracts and full-text of major astronomy and physics publications are indexed and searchable through the new ADS "Bumblebee" interface as well as the traditional "Classic" search forms. A set of browsable interfaces are also available.
Website	http://www.adsabs.harvard.edu/

Title	**ScholarsArchive /Brigham Young University**
Description	ScholarsArchive is Brigham Young University's institutional repository for the scholarly and creative content produced by the University. ScholarsArchive makes research, publications, data, and journals produced by BYU faculty and students available to a global research audience. Click here to submit to ScholarsArchive. The mission of ScholarsArchive is to support intensive learning, stimulating teaching, and excellent research by providing free, easy access to original scholarly and creative works produced by faculty, staff and students at Brigham Young University. In addition, ScholarsArchive hosts online journals and conferences published or managed by BYU departments. ScholarsArchive upholds the University's and Harold B. Lee Library's mission statements by simplifying the pursuit of lifelong learning and spiritual growth.
Website	http://scholarsarchive.byu.edu/

Title	Theses.fr
Description	theses.fr is a search engine to find French doctoral theses. theses.fr is an application resulting from the Portail des thèses project (or Theses Portal) commissioned to ABES in 2009 by the French Ministry for Higher Education and Research . Three majors aspects were included in the roadmap to: • strengthen national and international visibility of French doctoral research. theses.fr fully discloses on the web data describing these doctoral theses. • serve the academic community. theses.fr helps the whole scientific community to gain as accurate as possible a view into the state of ongoing doctoral research and to have an update on research being done on a subject or in a discipline. • serve the economy. By promoting the research done by doctoral students, theses.fr is also aimed at fostering the professional development of young researchers.
Website	http://www.theses.fr/

Title	Enlighten: Theses/ University of Glasgow
Description	All research postgraduate students are required to deposit one printed copy and one electronic copy of their thesis. This site provides full details of the process. The sections below provide details on what you need to do and the various aspects of the process you need to consider. Please read through each section before following the instructions on Depositing your thesis. If you need help with any aspect of the process please e-mail theses@gla.ac.uk. Please note that the regulations do not apply to Glasgow School of Art students, who should still submit two print copies of their thesis.
Website	http://theses.gla.ac.uk/

Title	Scholarship@Western
Description	Scholarship@Western is a multi-functional portal that collects, showcases, archives, and preserves a variety of materials created or sponsored by The University of Western Ontario community (hereinafter called Western). It aims to facilitate knowledge sharing and broaden the international recognition of Western's academic excellence by providing open access to Western's intellectual output and professional achievements. It also serves as a platform to support Western's scholarly communication needs and provides an avenue for the compliance of research funding agencies' open access policies.
Website	http://ir.lib.uwo.ca/

Title	Library of Auckland University
Description	The University of Auckland Library is the most extensive university library system in New Zealand and a national leader in the provision and development of digital resources. Search for University of Auckland theses. Also, the Library holds some theses from other universities, and provides access to hundreds of thousands of others online. There are many national and international websites and databases with lists of theses, some with full-text that you can download.
Website	http://www.library.auckland.ac.nz/services/research-support/finding-theses-and-dissertations

Title	Phd Data
Description	This site is the product of the combined initiative and efforts of several doctorate students in the U.S.A., Argentina and Israel, who felt the need for one site that would concentrate all existing information on doctoral researches around the world. All data supplied by applicants will be available to the �search� function, except personal email addresses that will be used for site management purposes only. Each applicant may register to the site on an individual basis and may change or terminate his/her registration through a secret password.
Website	http://www.phddata.org/index.php

Title	Qatar University institutional repository
Description	The Qatar University institutional repository aims to increase visibility of the original research and scholarly works of the QU community on a local and global level, capture the academic activities of QU, facilitate institutional academic achievement, and provide a permanent portal of access to resources for the QU community. The QU institutional repository is an online digital collection of scholarly output and academic activities. It includes faculty publications, research materials, learning materials, images, audio and video outputs, book chapters, reports and associated data, theses and dissertations, and conference proceedings.
Website	http://qspace.qu.edu.qa/

Title	Muhadharaty
Description	Lectures repository.
Website	https://www.muhadharaty.com/

Title	Dissertation
Description	Dissertation.com, an imprint of Universal-Publishers, was established in 1997 to provide students, researchers, and the general public with low cost access to important academic work. Since then, we have made hundreds of dissertations available online and through thousands of booksellers.
Website	http://dissertation.com/

Title	Legal Library
Description	Legal books and articles.
Website	http://www.legal-library-books.com/

Title	The Open University repository
Description	The Digital Archive of Research Theses (DART) has now been integrated into the University's research repository, Open Research Online (ORO). There is the option to browse theses or search for a specific thesis or theses within a subject area within ORO (check the theses box in the item type field and select and academic unit/department).
Website	http://www.open.ac.uk/library/library-resources/theses-dissertations

Title	**University of Leicester repository**
Description	Research publications and theses by members of the University of Leicester.
Website	https://lra.le.ac.uk/

Title	**University College of London repository**
Description	UCL Discovery is UCL's open access repository, showcasing and providing access to UCL research publications. To meet the requirements of the REF open access policy, UCL's publications policy and UCL's policy on thesis deposit, UCL researchers should upload all outputs to UCL's Research Publications Service (RPS). The open access team will make publications available in UCL Discovery according to the publisher's copyright permissions (usually after a delay period).
Website	http://discovery.ucl.ac.uk/

Title	Lisaanularab
Description	Free Books Blogger.
Website	http://lisaanularab.blogspot.hu/

Title	Books Jadid
Description	Free books website.
Website	http://www.booksjadid.info/#

Title	Asker Library
Description	Free books Library.
Website	http://ask2pdf.blogspot.hu/

Title	Mega Engineering Library
Description	Free engineering books, programs, courses, sheets, projects.
Website	http://www.megaenglib.com/

Title	Syrian Clinic
Description	Free Medical books.
Website	http://www.syrianclinic.com/website-content.html

Title	CORE
Description	CORE's mission is to aggregate all open access research outputs from repositories and journals worldwide and make them available to the public. In this way CORE facilitates free unrestricted access to research for all.
Website	https://core.ac.uk/

Title	Mouradonlayan
Description	Free books, programs, courses, projects.
Website	http://mouradonlayan.blogspot.hu/

Title	Swedish University Dissertations
Description	Dissertations.se lets you search among university dissertations from Sweden, written in English. At the moment there are 54055 finished dissertations in the database - and about half of these are available for download as PDF.
Website	http://www.dissertations.se/

Title	University of Reading PhD theses
Description	A selection of PhD thesis is listed, some of which are available online.
Website	https://www.reading.ac.uk/maths-and-stats/research/theses/maths-phdtheses.aspx

Title	King Saud University Repository
Description	Scientific production of King Saud University.
Website	http://repository.ksu.edu.sa/jspui/?locale=en

Title	Coursat
Description	Free courses website with variety of scientific topics.
Website	http://www.coursat.org/index.php

Title	The Institutional Repository of the University of South Carolina
Description	Scholar Commons is an Institutional Repository to preserve, collect and disseminate the research and scholarship of the University of South Carolina. With scholarly content contributed by faculty, researchers and students associated with the University, this repository will expand the visibility, access and influence of the University. It will also support efforts to increase collaboration and cross discipline research within the University and with other organizations. Contributions from authors include articles and books, documents, technical reports, presentations, conference proceedings, creative activities, master's theses, open-access dissertations and more. Scholar Commons is a service of the University Libraries that has been funded in part by the office of the CIO.
Website	http://scholarcommons.sc.edu/

Title	UKnowledge / University of Kentucky
Description	UKnowledge is a digital collection of unique scholarship created by University of Kentucky faculty, staff, students, departments, research centers, and administration. As a strategic initiative launched by UK Libraries to support multidisciplinary collaboration, UKnowledge is managed by specialists and sustained by dedicated funding. It captures, stores, organizes, and provides open and stable worldwide access to UK's intellectual capital, and also facilitates reuse of deposited materials to the extent warranted by copyright law or by the licensing terms of the concerned materials. Members of UK's academic community are encouraged to contribute their scholarship to UKnowledge.
Website	http://uknowledge.uky.edu/

Title	Iowa Research Online
Description	Iowa Research Online preserves and provides access to the research and creative scholarship created by the University of Iowa's faculty, students, and staff. The research papers, theses, dissertations, books, conference presentations, journals, and multimedia here represent Iowa's rich intellectual and cultural community.
Website	http://ir.uiowa.edu/

Title	ePublications@SCU
Description	ePublications@SCU is the institutional repository of Southern Cross University, highlighting the scholarly and creative works produced by SCU authors and researchers, as well as special collections managed by SCU Library.
Website	http://epubs.scu.edu.au/

Title	Iran Mavad
Description	Iranian website specialized in materials engineering.
Website	http://iran-mavad.com/

Title	SSRN Library
Description	SSRN's eLibrary provides 699,995 research papers from 322,843 researchers across 24 disciplines.
Website	https://www.ssrn.com/en/index.cfm?

Title	Mktba22
Description	Free books blogger.
Website	http://mktba22.blogspot.hu/

Title	Arabic legal library
Description	Free legal books, thesis, papers.
Website	http://bibliotdroit.blogspot.hu/

Title	NACA Archive
Description	Archive of National Advisory Committee for Aeronautics-NACA. Papers from 1917-1958.
Website	http://naca.central.cranfield.ac.uk/

Title	Handasaa 4 All
Description	Blogger specialized in engineering.
Website	http://handasaa4all.blogspot.hu/

Title	Books World
Description	Free Books Website.
Website	http://www.books-world.net/

Title	Getfreeebooks
Description	Getfreeebooks offered 10 Sites With Free German Ebooks Covering Over Thousands of Free Titles.
Website	http://www.getfreeebooks.com/10-sites-with-free-german-ebooks-covering-over-thousands-of-free-titles/

Title	Institutional Repositories/ University of Nebraska – Lincoln
Description	Institutional Repositories (IRs) bring together all of a University's research under one umbrella, with an aim to preserve and provide access to that research.
Website	http://digitalcommons.unl.edu/

Title	QScience
Description	QScience.com is the innovative and collaborative, peer-reviewed, online publishing platform from Hamad bin Khalifa University Press (HBKU Press). It offers a fast and transparent Open Access scholarly publishing process, which is centered on the author, bringing their research to a global audience.
Website	http://www.qscience.com/

Title	E-Books Directory
Description	E-Books Directory is a daily growing list of freely downloadable ebooks, documents and lecture notes found all over the internet. You can submit and promote your own ebooks, add comments on already posted books or just browse through the directory below and download anything you need.
Website	http://www.e-booksdirectory.com/

Title	Maktabatii
Description	Free Books Website.
Website	http://www.maktabatii.com/

Title	Strategic Net
Description	Free Papers, Projects Website.
Website	http://www.t1t.net/book/

Title	Open Access Journals Search Engine (OAJSE)
Description	Open Access Journals in the World.
Website	http://www.oajse.com/

Title	My Open Courses
Description	MOC evolved to provide access to quality education for skill development. We aim to empower the youth by providing cost effective learning solutions for skill development .
Website	http://myopencourses.com/

Title	Science Photo Library
Description	Science Photo Library (SPL) provides creative professionals with striking specialist imagery, unrivalled in quality, accuracy and depth of information. We have more than 600,000 images and 40,000 clips to choose from, with hundreds of new submissions uploaded to the website each week.
Website	http://www.sciencephoto.com/

Title	Trove/ Australian theses
Description	Trove is a free repository of Australian material, including almost a million Australian theses.
Website	http://www.caul.edu.au/caul-programs/australasian-digital-theses/finding-theses/trove-widgets

Title	James Cook University Theses
Description	James Cook University Masters and PhD theses and from other Australian universities.
Website	https://www.jcu.edu.au/library/find/books,-dvds-and-more/theses-collection/find-a-thesis

Title	E-Journal Database
Description	This resource provides users with access to your library's e-journals subscriptions via the EBSCOhost interface, bringing visibility to and increasing usage of your entire e-journal collection. The unique full text search limiter will return results for articles from both e-journals and databases subscribed to through EBSCO, ensuring that users have immediate access to all of the full-text content available in your collection.
Website	https://www.ebscohost.com/academic/e-journals-database

Title	Pakistan Research Repository
Description	Pakistan Research Repository is a project of the Higher Education Commission to promote the international visibility of research originating out of institutes of higher education in Pakistan. The aim of this service is to maintain a digital archive of all PhD theses produced indigenously to promote the intellectual output of Pakistani institutions. It provides a free, single-entry access point to view the manuscript of research executed, and distribute this information as widely as possible. The repository which is currently being populated with content has already made the full-text of PhD theses available in high-quality digitized format, whilst a further theses are in process of digitization. Higher Education Commission has introduced a systematic mechanism for the collection and digitization of all the theses produced so far in Pakistan
Website	http://eprints.hec.gov.pk/

Title	HighWire
Description	HighWire Press is the largest archive of free full-text science on Earth! As of 3/25/15, we are assisting in the online publication of 2,434,604 free full-text articles and 7,659,003 total articles. There are 41 sites with free trial periods, and 171 completely free sites.
Website	http://highwire.stanford.edu/lists/freeart.dtl

Title	Citeulike
Description	citeulike is a free service for managing and discovering scholarly references.
Website	http://www.citeulike.org/

Title	British Library e- theses online service
Description	Search over 400,000 doctoral theses. Download instantly for your research, or order a scanned copy quickly and easily.
Website	http://ethos.bl.uk/Home.do

Title	Open Access Theses and Dissertations
Description	OATD.org aims to be the best possible resource for finding open access graduate theses and dissertations published around the world. Metadata (information about the theses) comes from over 1100 colleges, universities, and research institutions. OATD currently indexes 3,426,292 theses and dissertations.
Website	https://oatd.org/

Title	National Center for Biotechnology Information
Description	The National Center for Biotechnology Information advances science and health by providing access to biomedical and genomic information.
Website	https://www.ncbi.nlm.nih.gov/

Title	Booksee
Description	Free books website.
Website	http://en.booksee.org/

Title	AZoM.com
Description	A novel concept in the field of Material Science publishing and information provision - AZoM.com (the A to Z of Materials) was formed with the primary aim of increasing the use of Advanced Materials by the engineering and design community worldwide. Tens of millions of engineers now use the internet as part of their daily lives, yet the vast majority of them are still unaware what can be achieved by the use of advanced ceramics, novel metallic alloys or state of the art composites. AZoM was built to change that.
Website	http://www.azom.com/

Title	OpenThesis
Description	OpenThesis is a free repository of theses, dissertations, and other academic documents, coupled with powerful search, organization, and collaboration tools.
Website	www.openthesis.org

Title	Quandl
Description	The World's Largest, Most Usable Collection of Free Financial and Economic Data
Website	https://www.quandl.com/open-data

Title	Open Culture Free Courses
Description	Get 1200 free online courses from the world's leading universities — Stanford, Yale, MIT, Harvard, Berkeley, Oxford and more.
Website	http://www.openculture.com/freeonlinecourses

Title	JURN
Description	JURN is a unique search tool which helps you find millions of free academic articles, chapters and theses.
Website	http://www.openculture.com/freeonlinecourses

Printed in Great Britain
by Amazon

51136441R00026